How to Buy
Platinum and Silver
for the Scrap Value

MGK

This book may help those who want to know how to test and buy scrap gold, platinum and silver. It may help people interested in starting their own business or become a collector.

Table of Contents

In order to buy gold, platinum and silver, you will need tools like those that are used by people in the trade of buying scrap gold, platinum and silver. These tools will help you assess the gold, platinum and silver you want to purchase. These tools will help you determine if the gold, platinum and silver are real, fake or plated. These tools will also help you determine the weight of the gold, platinum or silver and its fineness.

Many tools can be purchased on the internet or they may be for sale at your local jewelry supply store in your area. These tools should only be purchased and used by adults who have the ability to use them and store them with the knowledge and care to protect pets, children and others from harm.

Tools you will need to help you determine if the gold, platinum and silver are real, fake or plated and its weight are:

- **A testing stone**
- **A set of gold testing needles, containing one 10K, 14K, 18K, and 22K needle. You may also choose to purchase a silver testing needle.**
- **One bottle of each; 10K, 14K, 18K, 22K, Platinum and Silver Acid.**

These bottles of acid are premixed for what you are testing. (You may choose to wear acid resistant gloves to help protect you from any harmful effects from working with acid. You may want to wear protective eyewear, and test in a ventilated area.) You may also choose to use an electronic gold tester that does not use acid.

- A jeweler's loupe
- A scale that can weigh in pennyweights (dwt), troy ounces and grams (If you want the gram weight.)
- A file for filing small notches into the gold, platinum or silver being tested (For deeper testing into the metal). A triangular file would work.
- A magnet.
- A group of tools that you may already have at home (pliers, hammer, vise grips, small pocket knife, etc.) to help you take out of

the gold, platinum and silver any unwanted/unusable stones, watch parts or plaster that cannot be used or sold.

A testing stone is a black stone that you rub your gold onto it to test for the Karat of the gold and to test to see if it is gold. The most common types of Karats (K) of gold used in jewelry are 10K, 14K and 18K. There is jewelry made with less gold like 9K, and more gold like 22K.

One bottle of premixed testing acid for silver, one bottle for platinum, and one bottle for each gold Karat you want to be able to test. One bottle of silver acid, one bottle of platinum acid, one bottle of 10K acid, one bottle of 14K acid, one bottle of 18K acid, and one bottle of 22K acid. Using acid bottles with a drop applicator for testing gold, platinum and silver may be easier to use for testing.

If you are testing for 18K gold, after rubbing your gold item onto your testing stone. Place a drop of your 18K gold acid on the rubbed mark on the stone. The mark should remain unchanged. You may want to retest an unmarked piece of gold by using a higher Karat acid to check if it is a higher Karat. If it turned dark using the 18K acid you may want to try14K acid to see if it is 14K or less.

You may also choose to use an electronic gold tester that does not use acid. You may want to check and research the accuracy of the brand of the electronic gold tester before you purchase one.

If you want to be able to test for platinum and silver then you will need a premixed bottle of platinum acid and a premixed bottle of silver acid. If you are testing for platinum, rub your platinum item onto your testing stone. Place a drop of your Platinum acid on the rubbed mark on the stone. The mark should remain unchanged and stay a bright white in appearance for (.900) to (.999) pure platinum.

If you are testing for silver, rub your Silver item on your testing stone. Place a drop of your Silver acid on the rubbed mark on the stone. The mark should turn a creamy white color for silver that is (.900) to (.999) pure silver.

A set of gold testing needles is a set of needles with different Karats of gold on each tip. If you bought a set with 4 gold testing needles, one needle tip may be to test for 10K, another for 14K, another for 18K and another for 22K. Using the testing needles allow you to compare the gold you are testing to the Karat the needle shows by rubbing it onto your testing stone.

If you think you have a 14K ring and you want to check the gold Karat. You would rub the ring or whatever you are testing onto the stone. Then rub the 14K needle next to the ring mark on the stone. Place a drop of 14K acid onto both marks. Next, compare your marks. If the marks remain unchanged you will know that it is at least 14K gold.

You may want to retest an unmarked piece of gold by using a higher Karat acid to check if it is a higher Karat or if it turned dark using the 14K acid you may want to try10K acid to see if it is10K. After testing your gold by rubbing it onto the stone to determine the Karat, you may want to file a notch into the item and place a drop of acid onto the item to check as you did on the stone that there is no change to the gold and to make sure that it is not gold plated or gold filled.

A jeweler's loupe will help you be able to see the fine and worn stamped writing inside a piece of jewelry. It will help you to be able to see if a piece is stamped 14K, or 3 digit numbers like .583 or .750 that represents the fineness of the gold. The jeweler's loupe will also help you find imperfections in pieces like a broken prong, a cracked stone, a damaged watch or item.

A scale is an important tool that you will need. It will give you the weight of the item that you are looking at. A seller wants to sell you a 14K gold chain. How much should you pay for it? Does the chain weigh 10 pennyweights or 17 pennyweights? If you paid $20 per pennyweight for 17 pennyweights and found out later that it only weighed 10 pennyweights, then you over paid $140 for that item and may take a lost on the scrap value of the item. Weighing an item accurately will help you maximize profit and help you know what you are buying as a scrap buyer or collector.

Gold is often measured in pennyweights (dwt) for small items. There are 20 pennyweights to 1 troy ounce. 12 troy ounces equals 1 troy pound. Gold is also measured in grams. 1pennyweight is equal to 1.55 grams. 1 troy ounce is equal to 31.1 grams.

There are mechanical scales and electronic scales that you can use to weigh your gold. Electronic scales and mechanical scales vary in price. Electronic scales may be easier for some people to use and read the weight.

A file is used to make small notches on a hidden spot into the gold. A triangular file works well to file in small areas. This is done to test deeper into the gold to check if the object is gold plated (GP) heavy gold electroplated (HGE) or gold filled (GF).

You should not file a piece without the seller's permission and having an agreement with the seller what you will pay for the item if it is real prior to filing a notch and putting acid on the notch. You may want to have an agreement with the seller if it is not real gold. You may want to inform the seller that you will not buy the item if it is not gold, GF, GP, HGE or a low Karat gold less than 10K. You may also want to tell the seller that when you test the item by placing acid on the item, if it is not gold, GF, GP, HGE or a low Karat gold (Less than the testing acid) the item may be stained or damaged by the acid. You may want to tell the seller that you will not buy, repair or replace an item that is damaged by the acid or file as this is part of the testing procedure. If you see that an item is marked GF, GP, HGE, or a Karat of gold less than 10K you may choose not to test it because it is clearly marked and you know that based upon the markings, you are not going to buy it.

You may want to avoid melted gold nuggets, buttons and bars. These items may require them to be assayed by a refiner. The refiner will charge a fee to cover their work to determine the makeup of the gold nuggets, buttons and bars. It could be made up of a variety of gold Karats, silver and other metals mixed in. You will need to contact a refiner in order to determine the costs of the assay. Then determine if you have enough material there that is worth the costs. Then who is going to pay for the assay, you, the customer, or both? You may also have to consider the risk that the assay can come back with bad results with cost of the assay eliminating any profit or creating a loss.

A magnet will help in identifying gold, platinum and silver as they are not magnetic. A magnet will not be able to pick up gold, platinum or silver.

A group of tools that you may already have at home (pliers, hammer, small pocket knife, vise grips, etc.) to help you take out of the gold, platinum and silver unwanted/unusable stones, watch parts and plaster. Some gold medallions are filled with shellac. Some silverware candles holders and other items are filled with plaster to give them weight. If you are buying an item for the scrap value only then you don't want to pay for items filled with plaster. The plaster will make the item heavier than it really is and you only want to pay for the gold, platinum or silver because that is what you will be paid for. You should not damage an item prior to having an agreed upon price with the seller for the item.

There are gem stones and diamonds that you do not want to damage when removing these items from your scrap. These items can be sold to a gem stone buyer or diamond buyer. The sale of these items may be based upon size and quality. The value would be determined by the gem stone buyer, diamond buyer, or a professional appraisal. If you think you have an expensive diamond or gem stone, you may want to have it checked out first by the gem stone buyer or diamond buyer. Let them buy it from you or have a professional like a diamond setter remove the stone until you are ready to sell the diamond or gem stone.

Testing Stone

Gold Testing Needles

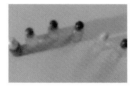

Bottles of Acid

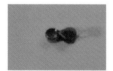

Jeweler's Loupe

Electronic Scale

Buying Gold, Platinum and Silver for the Scrap Value

When you have your tools to aid you in identifying and making a purchase of gold, platinum and silver for the scrap value, you need to figure out how much are you going to pay for it. The scrap value of gold, platinum and silver is the melt value of the item by its weight. The items condition does not matter. It can be crushed, broken, missing pieces, coins, or in perfect condition, you are paying for it based upon the scrap value. In order to buy gold, platinum and silver for the scrap value, you need to know what the price of gold, platinum or silver is selling for on that day. There are sources that you can get this information, from your local gold buying dealer, refiner, coin collector, jeweler and on the web from a reputable site.

Once you know what the price of gold, platinum or silver is selling for on the day you are going to buy your scrap. You will need to know how much you will be receiving from the business you are selling to in order to determine your profit margin. You may want to find out what they will pay you on the day you plan on buying from your customer. The company you sell to may have their own price policy paying anywhere from 60% to 98% of the scrap value. Some companies have a flat rate dollar amount that they pay. You may find it easier to sell your scrap to a gold buying dealer or refiner that will pay you by a percentage based upon the price of gold for that day. You may find that the more you have to sell the higher percentage you might receive from your buyer. Many places won't pay the high percentages like 90% and above for a low volume of weight. The price you receive may be based upon the price you negotiate with your buyer or their standard price policy.

Once you know the amount you will receive from your buyer, you can now determine how much you will be willing to pay for an item from your customer. If you know that your buyer will pay you 90% of the value of the gold based upon the market price. You may choose to pick a range from 50% to 75% to offer your customer. You will also need to determine the cost to compete in your area. If your competitors are paying 50% of the scrap value, then you may choose to pay the same amount or a little more.

This is an example only because since this is your business you will need to choose your own profit margin. You will also need to take in account your own business and overhead costs.

In order to buy gold, platinum and silver for the scrap value, you will also need to know the value of the fineness of the item. The gold that some dentist uses in some of their work is 16K. Many coins are 90% to 99% gold or silver, but there are coins on the market that contains less than 90% or contain no gold or silver.

10K which is .417 or 41.7 % gold has less gold content than 18K which is .750 or 75 % gold. Therefore, it is worth less and you should pay less for it.

Fineness of Gold, Platinum and Silver

Gold Karat   =   % of Gold Content

24K	=	.999
22K	=	.917
21K	=	.875
20K	=	.833
18K	=	.750
16K	=	.667
14K	=	.583
10K	=	.417

Silver   % of Silver Content

Silver-Pure	=	.999
Sterling Silver (Ster)	=	.925

Platinum

Platinum-Pure   =   .999

Platinum (Pt) or (Plat) =   .950

Platinum (Pt) or (Plat) =   .900

Price of Gold, Platinum and Silver

Now that you understand the fineness of gold, platinum and silver, you will look at the price of 1 ounce of gold, platinum and silver and the price of each by the pennyweight (dwt.) For example, if the price of gold was $1870.65 per ounce on a given day. You would know how to get the price gold by the pennyweight per Karat. To do this you would take the price of gold $1870.65 and the multiply it by the % of the Karat gold content and then divide it by 20 (dwt).

Examples: (Both examples give the same answer)

$1870.65 × .750 ÷ 20 = $70.15   Price × % of Content ÷20 = $

(or)

$$\frac{\$1870.65 \times .750 = \$70.15}{20} \qquad \frac{\text{Price} \times \text{\% of Content} = \$}{20}$$

$70.15 is the price per pennyweight for 18K gold at 100% of its value based upon the price at $1870.65. You can use this formula to determine the price per pennyweight of gold, platinum and silver.

Gold Karat	% of Gold Content	Price of Gold per (DWT) 100%
22K	.917	$85.77
18K	.750	$70.15
14K	.583	$54.53
10K	.417	$39.00

Platinum	% of Platinum Content	Price of Platinum per (DWT) 100%
		(Example price on a given day)
$1500 per ounce	.950	$71.25
	.900	$67.50

Silver	% of Silver Content	Price of Silver per (DWT) 100%
		(Example price on a given day)
$30 per ounce	.925	$1.38

Converting Price into Profit

Once you know the price per pennyweight of the gold, platinum or silver you want to buy, you can now determine the price you will be receiving from your buyer. You can also determine the price you want to pay a seller.

The price you know now is the full market price of the gold, platinum and silver. If you are being paid for example 90% of the market price from your buyer, then you need to be able to figure out that amount. You can do this by using the formula based upon the known price of the content of the gold, platinum or silver.

For example, you know that the price of 18K gold per pennyweight is $70.15, based upon a gold selling price of $1870.65 per ounce. $70.15 per pennyweight is 100% of the value. If you are being paid by your gold buyer or refiner 90% of the percent of content, then you will need to figure out the value of 90%. To determine what you will be paid by your buyer you would multiply the price of 100% x 90%= your price.

Example:
$70.15 × .90 = $63.14 per (dwt.)

This is the amount you will receive from your buyer.

If you pay 50% to your seller, **$70.15×.50 = <u>$35.08 per (dwt.)</u>**

This is the amount you may choose to pay your seller. You may choose to pay more than 50 % in a very competitive area.

$63.14 - $35.08 = <u>$28.06 per (dwt.)</u>

Based upon this example you will make a profit of $28.06 per (dwt.) If you bought 20 pennyweights from this one seller, ($28.06 × 20 = $561.20) you would make a profit of $561.20.

This is an example only because since this is your business you will need to choose your own profit margin. You will also need to take in account your own business and overhead costs. After buying your scrap gold, platinum or silver from your customer, you may want to sell it because the price may drop the next day. It could also go up, but that is taking a risk.

The price you got from your buyer and the price you gave to your customer were based upon the day's quote you got from your buyer. If the day's quote you got from your buyer was based upon the price of gold being $1870.65 per ounce, and tomorrow the gold price fell to $1770.65 then you would probably receive a lower price and quote from your buyer based upon the lower price of gold on the day you sold it to your buyer.

Review of the Steps to Buying Gold, Platinum and Silver for the Scrap Value

- Get the tools for testing, weighing, protecting, and breaking out unwanted parts for scrap.
- Get the days selling price of the gold, platinum or silver, and find out what your buyer will pay you.
- Determine what you will pay your customer and what your profit margin will be.
- Test the items to determine if you have gold, platinum or silver and its fineness.
- Weigh the amount you have by it fineness after breaking out unwanted parts for scrap. If you think you have an expensive diamond or gem, you may want to have it checked out first by a diamond or gem stone buyer and let them buy it from you or have a professional like a diamond setter remove the stone until you are ready to sell the diamond or gem stone.
- After buying it from your customer, sell it because the price may drop the next day. It could also go up, but you would be taking that risk.

Suggestions on Where You May Find Scrap Gold, Platinum and Silver to Buy

Now that you know how to buy scrap gold, platinum and silver, you may be wondering where you may find it. This book is written for the purpose of how to buy scrap gold, platinum and silver. Marketing and servicing your business as an owner or collector is the decisions you will have to make yourself. The following is only suggestions that may help you get started, with no guarantees of success.

You may choose to advertise locally and have people call you if they have something to sell. You will have to make arrangements where to meet for the transaction. You can give scrap gold, platinum and silver buying parties. You can travel to retail locations like antique shops, jewelry stores, flea markets, dental offices, coin dealers and thrift shops and ask if they have any scrap gold, platinum or silver to sell.

You can advertise in your local paper, flyers, word of mouth, or on the internet. You can set up a booth at a flea market, open an office, rent part of a retail space, or open a retail location. You should check your local laws to see if you need a license to operate your business.

Again, marketing and servicing your business as an owner or collector is the decisions you will have to make yourself.

MGK
©

39678566R00016

Printed in Poland
by Amazon Fulfillment
Poland Sp. z o.o., Wrocław